Freight Trucks

Julie Murray

Abdo Kids Junior
is an Imprint of Abdo Kids
abdobooks.com

TRUCKS AT WORK

abdobooks.com

Published by Abdo Kids, a division of ABDO, P.O. Box 398166, Minneapolis, Minnesota 55439. Copyright © 2024 by Abdo Consulting Group, Inc. International copyrights reserved in all countries. No part of this book may be reproduced in any form without written permission from the publisher. Abdo Kids Junior™ is a trademark and logo of Abdo Kids.

Printed in the United States of America, North Mankato, Minnesota.

052023

092023

THIS BOOK CONTAINS RECYCLED MATERIALS

Photo Credits: Getty Images, Shutterstock

Production Contributors: Teddy Borth, Jennie Forsberg, Grace Hansen

Design Contributors: Candice Keimig, Pakou Moua

Library of Congress Control Number: 2022946718

Publisher's Cataloging-in-Publication Data

Names: Murray, Julie, author.

Title: Freight trucks / by Julie Murray

Description: Minneapolis, Minnesota : Abdo Kids, 2024 | Series: Trucks at work | Includes online resources and index.

Identifiers: ISBN 9781098266158 (lib. bdg.) | ISBN 9781098266851 (ebook) | ISBN 9781098267209 (Read-to-me ebook)

Subjects: LCSH: Trucks--Juvenile literature. | Vehicles--Juvenile literature. | Truck freight--Juvenile literature.

Classification: DDC 388.32--dc23

Table of Contents

Freight Trucks 4

More
Freight Trucks 22

Glossary. 23

Index 24

Abdo Kids Code. 24

Freight Trucks

Freight trucks move things from one place to another.

5

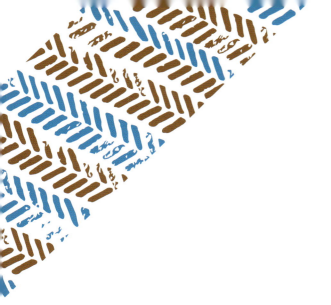

Different trucks and trailers **haul** different things.

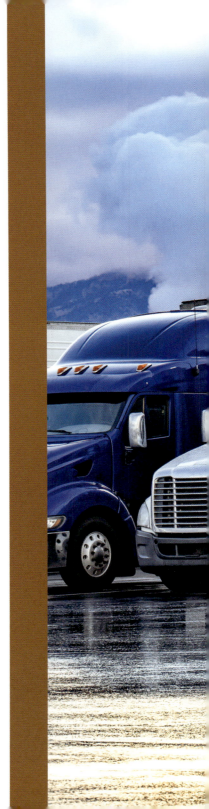

Special trucks keep cargo cold.

Refrigeration truck

Flatbeds are open. They can move large amounts of heavier items.

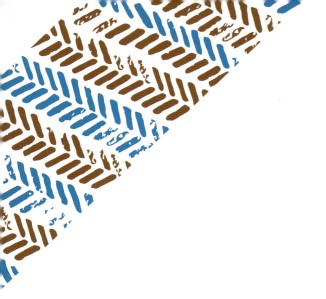

Drop decks sit lower to the ground. They carry items too tall for flatbeds.

Dry van trucks protect cargo. They can carry up to 45,000 pounds (20,000 kg)!

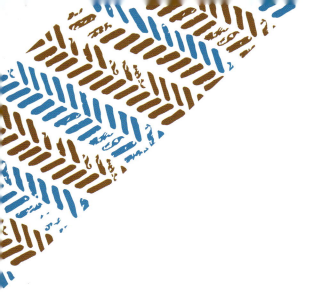

Box trucks can carry larger items. They are often used for deliveries.

Tanker trucks carry liquid.

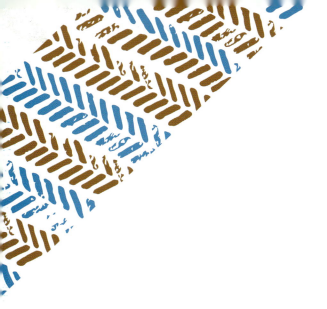

What is your favorite **freight** truck?

More Freight Trucks

auto carrier

curtain truck

dry bulk tanker

tipper truck

Glossary

freight
goods shipped in bulk. Cargo is another word for freight.

haul
to carry goods from one place to another.

Index

box truck 16

drop deck 12

dry van 14

flatbed 10

refrigerated truck 8

tanker truck 18

uses 4, 6, 8, 10, 12, 14, 16, 18

Visit **abdokids.com** to access crafts, games, videos, and more!

Use Abdo Kids code **TFK6158** or scan this QR code!